EAT LI!
BOOK SE]

Eat Like a Local- Sarasota: Sarasota Florida Food Guide

I have lived in the Sarasota area since 1998 and learned about many great places that I want to try. –Conoal

Eat Like a Local: Connecticut: Connecticut Food Guide

This a great guide to try different places in Connecticut to eat. Can't wait to try them all! The author is awesome to explore and try all these different foods/drinks. There are places I didn't know they existed until I got this book and I am a CT resident myself! –Caroline J. H.

Eat Like a Local: Las Vegas: Las Vegas Nevada Food Guide

Perfect food guide for any tourist traveling to Vegas or any local looking to go outside their comfort zone! – TheBondes

Eat Like a Local-Jacksonville: Jacksonville Florida Food Guide

Loved the recommendations. Great book from someone who knows their way around Jacksonville. –Anonymous

Eat Like a Local- Costa Brava: Costa Brava Spain Food Guide

The book was very well written. Visited a few of the restaurants in the book, they were great! Sylvia V.

Eat Like a Local-Sacramento: Sacramento California Food Guide

As a native of Sacramento, Emerald's book touches on some of our areas premier spots for food and fun. She skims the surface of what Sacramento has to offer recommending locations in historical, popular areas where even more jewels can be found. –Katherine G.

EAT LIKE A LOCAL- BOSTON

Boston Massachusetts Food Guide

Nicolette Degrassi

Eat Like a Local- Boston Copyright © 2022 by CZYK Publishing LLC. All Rights Reserved.

All rights reserved. No part of this book may be reproduced in any form or by any electronic or mechanical means including information storage and retrieval systems, without permission in writing from the author. The only exception is by a reviewer, who may quote short excerpts in a review.

The statements in this book are of the authors and may not be the views of CZYK Publishing.

Cover designed by: Lisa Rusczyk Ed. D.

CZYK Publishing Since 2011.
CZYKPublishing.com
Eat Like a Local

Mill Hall, PA
All rights reserved.
ISBN: 9798353642275

BOOK DESCRIPTION

Are you excited about planning your next trip? Do you want an edible experience? Would you like some culinary guidance from a local? If you answered yes to any of these questions, then this Eat Like a Local book is for you. Eat Like a Local, Boston by Nicolette Degrassi offers the inside scoop on some of the best restaurants Boston has to offer. Culinary tourism is an important aspect of any travel experience. Food has the ability to tell you a story of a destination, its landscapes, and culture on a single plate. Most food guides tell you how to eat like a tourist. Although there is nothing wrong with that, as part of the Eat Like a Local series, this book will give you a food guide from someone who has lived at your next culinary destination.

In these pages, you will discover advice on having a unique edible experience. This book will not tell you exact addresses or hours but instead will give you excitement and knowledge of food and drinks from a local that you may not find in other travel food guides.

Eat like a local. Slow down, stay in one place, and get to know the food, people, and culture. By the time you finish this book, you will be eager and prepared to travel to your next culinary destination.

OUR STORY

Traveling has always been a passion of the creator of the Eat Like a Local book series. During Lisa's travels in Malta, instead of tasting what the city offered, she ate at a large fast-food chain. However, she realized that her traveling experience would have been more fulfilling if she had experienced the best of local cuisines. Most would agree that food is one of the most important aspects of a culture. Through her travels, Lisa learned how much locals had to share with tourists, especially about food. Lisa created the Eat Like a Local book series to help connect people with locals which she discovered is a topic that locals are very passionate about sharing. So please join me and: Eat, drink, and explore like a local.

TABLE OF CONTENTS

Eat Like a Local-
Book Series Reviews
BOOK DESCRIPTION
OUR STORY
TABLE OF CONTENTS
DEDICATION
ABOUT THE AUTHOR
HOW TO USE THIS BOOK
FROM THE PUBLISHER
Before we Begin…
1. Getting Around the City
2. Show Me the Money
3. Read Reviews
4. Book a Reservation
5. Grab a Cup of Coffee
6. Best Brunch with a View
7. Best Boozy Brunch
8. Donut forget about fried dough
9. Pack a Picnic
10. Grab a Slice
11. Binge on some BBQ
12. Get a Lobster Roll
13. Did someone say ceviche?
14. Order Oysters

15. Eat the Meat
16. Leave the Meat
17. I Scream, You Scream, We All Scream for Vegan Ice Cream
18. Expand your horizons
19. Craving Cuban?
20. Dumpling Crawl through Chinatown
21. Explore Eastie's Colombian Dining Scene
22. Sip Greek Wine
23. Get Cotton Candy at the Mexican Mainstay
24. Splurge on Sushi
25. Sample Spanish Small Plates
26. Tunes and Tapas
27. Try Vietnamese in Dorchester
28. Craft Cocktails Meet Chinese Food
29. Ramen in Brookline
30. More in Coolidge Corner
31. See and Be Seen
32. Dine Like a Parisian
33. Another South End Favorite
34. Farm-to-Table at its Finest
35. Seasonal Favorites in Somerville
36. Eat Pasta in Boston's Little Italy
37. Sip on an Espresso Martini
38. Cannoli Crawl through the North End
39. Grab a Pint

40. Cheers to more beer!
41. Experience Cocktail Artistry
42. Visit a Speakeasy
43. Stop at Fenway for a Frank
44. Taste Test at a Food Market
45. More Market Munchies
46. Don't Forget Food Trucks
47. Go to the place where "Everybody Knows Your Name"
48. Take a Cooking Class
49. Visit the Oldest Restaurant in the City
50. End with some History

Why You Should Book this Trip

READ OTHER BOOKS BY

CZYK PUBLISHING

DEDICATION

This book is dedicated to my best friend, Maggie. Thank you for always encouraging my curiosity and supporting my creative endeavors. Your zest for life and eternal optimism are unparalleled. Thank you for being my partner in life and the person who feeds my soul (and belly).

ABOUT THE AUTHOR

Nicolette is a freelance writer, traveler, and food fanatic. She was born and raised in New York but moved to Boston after graduating from Stonehill College in Easton, Massachusetts. She has resided in Boston for over ten years and is consistently looking for new restaurants to fuel her food obsession.

When Nicolette was 16 years old, her aunt and uncle took her on a two-week tour through Italy that ignited her passion for travel (and food). She is curious by nature and loves to experience new things. She believes sharing similar experiences with others is the best way to connect and, as such, is always willing to share her travel itineraries. Her favorite trips are the ones that immerse her in the culture of a new city and allow her to experience things the way that locals do. She took on freelance writing to document her travels and reflect on her favorite memories.

HOW TO USE THIS BOOK

The goal of this book is to help culinary travelers either dream or experience different edible experiences by providing opinions from a local. The author has made suggestions based on their own knowledge. Please do your own research before traveling to the area in case the suggested locations are unavailable.

Travel Advisories: As a first step in planning any trip abroad, check the Travel Advisories for your intended destination.
https://travel.state.gov/content/travel/en/traveladvisories/traveladvisories.html

FROM THE PUBLISHER

Traveling can be one of the most important parts of a person's life. The anticipation and memories that you have are some of the best. As a publisher of the *Eat Like a Local*, Greater Than a Tourist, as well as the popular *50 Things to Know* book series, we strive to help you learn about new places, spark your imagination, and inspire you. Wherever you are and whatever you do I wish you safe, fun, and inspiring travel.

Lisa Rusczyk Ed. D.
CZYK Publishing

Eat Like a Local

"Food is our common ground, a universal experience."

– James Beard.

For me, Boston is the perfect combination of old and new. While the city has managed to preserve its history, it is also constantly evolving and diversifying, allowing me to experience new cultures in my own city. Whether you're new to town or a lifelong resident, there is much to explore.

Boston's food scene has significantly progressed over the years, offering various cuisines that can satisfy every palette. While this coastal city is home to top-notch seafood restaurants, it also has a plethora of international dishes from every corner of the globe. Foodies no longer refer to Boston as "bean town" because the food scene here has become more refined and broadened immensely.

All over the world, people say they make friends by "breaking bread together." Food is something that really helps to connect people and allows us to immerse ourselves into different cultures. One of my favorite pastimes is uncovering new restaurants throughout the many neighborhoods of Boston. My restaurant bucket list is constantly growing. From cozy cafes to secret speakeasies to the freshest farm-to-table restaurants, I always manage to find new dining experiences that bring me back for more and allow me to share with others.

While Boston has much to offer, I have tried my best to compile a list of the best eateries in the city. I hope these suggestions and tips allow you to appreciate Boston as much as I have over the years.

BEFORE WE BEGIN...

It is important to note that Boston has many neighborhoods, each with their own distinct characteristics and often tied to specific cuisines. For instance, Italian food takes center stage in the North End. Meanwhile, East Boston is known for its collection of Colombian establishments. Yet, no matter where you go, there will be something for everyone. Below is a map of the city for easy reference so you can familiarize yourself with the neighborhoods of Boston as well as some noteworthy suburbs you should keep in mind.

Eat Like a Local

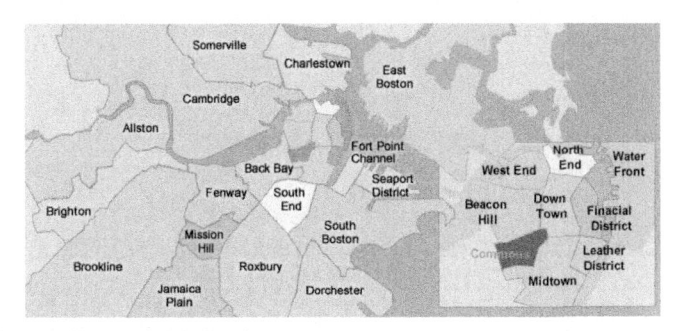

Photo credit: 3DAPARTMENT team

Boston
Massachusetts, USA

11

Boston Massachusetts Climate

	High	Low
January	37	22
February	39	24
March	46	31
April	57	41
May	67	50
June	77	59
July	82	66
August	81	65
September	73	58
October	62	47
November	52	38
December	42	28

GreaterThanaTourist.com

Temperatures are in Fahrenheit degrees.
Source: NOAA

Eat Like a Local

1. GETTING AROUND THE CITY

Boston is an old city where the roads were built around houses, so the streets can sometimes be hard to navigate via car. Luckily, Boston is a very walkable city for those who want to get their steps in. Suppose you're planning to visit different neighborhoods in Boston. In that case, you can use the MBTA or "T, " the subway system running throughout the city. Trains typically run every 5-15 minutes, making it a convenient way to travel. Fare for the T is $2.25 per ride with a CharlieCard, which can be purchased at self-service kiosks at any station. If you want to bring a car, metered parking is an option in most neighborhoods, as is parking in garages for the day. The app SpotHero is an excellent tool for finding available and cheap parking throughout the city. Finally, ride sharing apps such as Uber and Lyft are commonplace in Boston. If you'd prefer to use these, you can easily order a car within 5-10 minutes.

2. SHOW ME THE MONEY

Nearly every Boston coffee shop, restaurant, and convenience store accept credit cards. You only need cash for the occasional street market purchase or a handful of restaurants in the North End that are cash only. Many establishments also accept electronic payment via phones and watches. So long as you have your credit card information handy, you should be good to go. As for tipping, most restaurants include tip percentages at the bottom of their checks. If you are unfamiliar with how to tip, 18% of your total bill is standard, however 20-25% is recommended.

3. READ REVIEWS

While I like to think that my own palette is refined, everyone's taste buds are different. Reading online reviews before booking a reservation is a great way to see photos of the food you may order, what customers thought of the service, and whether they'd return. Take a few minutes to examine ratings, pros, and cons to determine which restaurant best suits you and your group. While you're at it, look up restaurants on social media. I'll admit, half of the restaurants on my to-do list were found via Instagram. I am a sucker for a good photo and a caption highlighting a unique or fun dining experience. Besides, if you didn't post it, did it even happen?

4. BOOK A RESERVATION

Generally, you'll be able to find somewhere to eat on short notice in Boston. Still, there are certain restaurants you'll want to book a reservation for in advance – especially during peak dining hours. There are a handful of restaurants in Boston proper that are notoriously busy and will require planning ahead. But if you can't get a reservation for your desired spot, a little flexibility goes a long way. At most restaurants, you may have luck showing up right as they open and grabbing a seat at the bar. Many restaurants serve their full menu at the bar, so you don't need a formal table to enjoy a meal.

5. GRAB A CUP OF COFFEE

While I am partial to tea, many people like to start their day with a cup of coffee. There are many great cafés in Boston, but one of the most aesthetic places to grab a coffee is **Tatte Bakery**. This instagrammable bakery and café is a chain that can be found scattered around the city. Between rich coffee aromas, modern furnishings, and a bright, open concept space, Tatte offers an inviting sit-down environment for its customers. Their drink menu rivals other coffee shops in the area. Their iced vanilla latte provides the perfect combination of espresso and vanilla flavors. The pastry counter is lined with delectable desserts such as buttery croissants, crème brulé, and chocolate hazelnut brioche. But Tatte is not just a pastry place. It also has an extensive menu of sandwiches, hearty salads, and several Israeli-inspired items like three different types of shakshuka and a Fattoush salad.

6. BEST BRUNCH WITH A VIEW

Perched atop The Newbury Boston hotel, **Contessa** is an elevated dining experience featuring floor to ceiling windows, luscious plants, and cozy seating. At Contessa visitors are offered sweeping views of Back Bay and the Boston Public Garden as they enjoy an elegant, Italian-inspired brunch. Order traditional breakfast items such as a Florentine benedict, Panettone French toast, or avocado bruschetta trapanese. For heartier options, their burrata, squash carpaccio, or pizza del giorno will satisfy any appetite. As for cocktails, you'll find an array of Italian-inspired cocktails such as spritzes and negronis. If you want to try something more unique, order the Sgroppino, featuring lemon vodka and sorbet or the Boston Sour made with Irish whiskey, egg white, lemon, and Lambrusco.

7. BEST BOOZY BRUNCH

Arguably one of the best places to grab a boozy brunch is at **Lincoln Tavern & Restaurant** in South Boston. From a stack of Fruity Pebble pancakes to dark chocolate waffles, this restaurant goes above and beyond to create exceptional brunch options. And they don't just offer brunch on the weekends – you can also order your favorite breakfast treats during the weekday. However, the real treat at Lincoln is ordering a bucket of bubbles to get your weekend off to a sparkling start. The infamous bucket of bubbles comes with a bottle of Prosecco and an assortment of juices (grapefruit, orange juice, and apple cider) so that you can make your own mimosas to pair with brunch. One thing to note is that the weekend and weekday brunch menus are different, so make sure to check their website if your heart is set on a particular dish.

8. DONUT FORGET ABOUT FRIED DOUGH

Follow the smell of fried dough and satisfy your sweet tooth with a donut from **Union Square Donuts**. This popular bakery churns out donuts that are soft, airy, and full of flavor. A roster of classic options such as glazed, Boston cream, and rainbow sprinkles are always available, but the bakers at Union Square Donuts have a knack for pushing the boundaries of creative flavors. Experiment with flavors like maple bacon, sea-salt whiskey caramel, or orange creamsicle (a summertime special). They also serve donut holes as well some vegan options. Union Square Donuts has several locations in Somerville, Brookline, and Boston.

9. PACK A PICNIC

The Charles River Esplanade is a stunning riverfront park that runs through the city of Boston. On any given day, it is not uncommon to find people enjoying a picnic along the water. Grab an oversized blanket and some groceries from any local grocery store (Trader Joes or Whole Foods are typically my preference) and have yourself a picnic with breathtaking views. For something a bit fancier, head to **Kured** in Beacon Hill and pick up a charcuterie box (assorted cold meats and cheeses) to enjoy with a special someone or a group of friends. Kured offers pre-made box options, but you can also choose your own. Each box includes three types of meats, three kinds of cheese, and three sides. All their ingredients are locally sourced and can be customized to accommodate dietary restrictions such as vegetarian, pork-free, or Keto friendly.

10. GRAB A SLICE

While Boston may not be known for its pizza, there is one pizzeria in the North End you should not miss: **Regina Pizzeria**. Opened in 1926, Regina is not only the oldest pizzeria in town but has become one of the most beloved. If you don't believe me, you'll believe the long line of patrons waiting outside its doors. Come here to grab a pie and a pitcher and soak up its movie-set-like interior with distressed booths and celebrity headshots hung on the walls. For an authentic Regina experience, order the giambotta pizza, which includes all of the traditional toppings – sausage, pepperoni, salami, onions, mushrooms, peppers, and anchovies. While Regina is now a nationally recognized local chain, the original outpost on Thacher Street is worth visiting for its no-frills, brick oven pizza.

11. BINGE ON SOME BBQ

From beef brisket to fried chicken, **Sweet Cheeks Q** in Fenway is one of the best barbeque joints in the city. Chef Tiffani Faison offers authentic Texas barbeque staples and delicious southern sides. The restaurant has a casual atmosphere with food piled onto metal trays and patrons seated at family-style tables. This is a place to indulge. Try their bucket of biscuits paired with honey butter or fried green tomatoes alongside your carefully smoked ribs. For dessert, try their giant Nutter Butter cookie: two large peanut butter sugar cookies held together by a sweet, whipped peanut butter filling.

12. GET A LOBSTER ROLL

It would be a mistake to visit Boston without ordering a lobster roll. The warm lobster roll at **Neptune Oyster** is a contender for the best in the city. This iconic North End restaurant is one you should not miss. However, the space is small, and the restaurant does not take reservations. To snag a spot at the marble-filled oyster bar, you will most likely have to wait in line. But the lobster roll is worth it. You'll be rewarded with heaps of chunky lobster meat on a grilled brioche bun slathered in warm butter or mayo. Pro tip: try visiting Neptune Oyster mid-afternoon on a weekday or arrive before the doors open on a weekend to avoid the crazy lines.

13. DID SOMEONE SAY CEVICHE?

Celeste is a cozy little restaurant in Somerville's Union Square that celebrates Peruvian cuisine. Co-founders JuanMa Calderón and Maria Rondeau have created an inviting space that feels more like an intimate dinner party with friends rather than a restaurant full of strangers. Their menu showcases home-cooked Peruvian classics. Come here for a variety of vibrant ceviche options and fragrant entrees such as camaron al ajillo (shrimp scampi) and lomo saltado (stir-fried beef sirloin). The cocktail menu focuses on mezcal and pisco, but they also serve wine. The maracuya sour is particularly delicious if you like passionfruit. So, find a seat at the bar and watch their open kitchen create pure Peruvian magic.

14. ORDER OYSTERS

Possibly some of the best seafood in the city can be found at **Row 34**. Located in Fort Point, this self-proclaimed "workingman's oyster bar" offers some of the freshest oysters in Boston. Their raw bar features an extensive oyster selection from locations scattered throughout New England. Obviously, make sure to try the Row 34s from Duxbury, by which the restaurant is named after. The team at Row 34 love beer as much as they do oysters so be sure to pair your oysters with a glass of one of their recommended craft beers. If you're particularly hungry, order a warm buttered lobster roll too. It will quite literally melt in your mouth. Due to the restaurants increasing popularity, reservations are hard to come by so plan accordingly.

15. EAT THE MEAT

Tucked away in the historic Beacon Hill is one of the most distinguished steakhouses in Boston: **Mooo**. This modern steakhouse prides itself on offering a relaxed yet sophisticated atmosphere, high-end premium cuts, and an extensive wine list of over 325 labels. Come here to indulge in a tender 12-ounce filet mignon or a 24-ounce bone-in Delmonico. Their meats are delicate and juicy and cooked to perfection. Pair your meat with a side of creamed spinach or roasted cauliflower. Or, if you've worked up an appetite, add on clams, Maine lobster, or a grilled branzino. No matter what you choose, you won't be disappointed at Mooo. One bit of advice: Mooo is on the more expensive side, so make sure you are ready to splurge. They also have a sister location in the Seaport.

16. LEAVE THE MEAT

Vegetarian restaurants have become more prevalent in Boston. If you love food but don't eat meat, there are several great options for you to try. **Grasshopper** in Allston is one of Boston's better-known restaurants that serve vegan Chinese food. Vegans and vegetarians alike flock to this pan-Asian establishment to experience comfort food without the meat. Choose from a selection of vegetarian dumplings, spring rolls, and stir-fried greens. Their tofu and seitan dishes imitate meat dishes so well that you'll get the full Chinese food fix. Their "no-name" dish is crowd favorite: battered seitan dipped in a sweet and sour sauce and served with an assortment of steam veggies.

17. I SCREAM, YOU SCREAM, WE ALL SCREAM FOR VEGAN ICE CREAM

Plant-based ice cream can be tricky to perfect. Still, **FoMu** does a fantastic job of creating ice "cream" without sacrificing the smooth consistency or rich flavors of traditional ice cream. If you are vegan or just love ice cream but can't handle dairy, FoMu has you covered. Their ice cream is made from scratch with coconut milk and carefully sourced, plant-based ingredients. Try grasshopper pie made from natural green peppermint and dark chocolate chunks or venture out and try an offbeat flavor like avocado. No matter what your preference, this place has a flavor for everyone. You can also pick up smoothies, frappes, and other non-dairy desserts. FoMu has multiple locations throughout Boston, including Fenway, South End, Allston, and Jamacia Plain.

18. EXPAND YOUR HORIZONS

Boston's food scene offers an abundance of international cuisines that can satisfy every palette. Looking to cozy up with an exotic blend of Mediterranean food? **Oleana** in Cambridge, Massachusetts, is a must-try eatery with majestic vibes and exquisite plates rich in flavor. Executive chef Ana Sortun is known around the Boston area for her spice-forward cuisine, drawing inspiration from Turkey, Lebanon, and Greece. Oleana's meze-styled plates are made with the freshest ingredients, grown locally at Siena Farms, owned by Sortun and her husband. Seductive flavors combined with a commitment to fresh ingredients make Oleana a restaurant you won't want to miss. Fan favorites include the spinach falafel and lamb moussaka.

And while you're at it, try some other exceptional cuisines…

Eat Like a Local

19. CRAVING CUBAN?

Located two blocks from Porter Square in Cambridge is **Gustazo**, a restaurant that speaks to the Cuban heritage. Gustazo, which translates to "great pleasure," is a slice of Havana in the city. Their menu boasts a variety of exquisite tapas. Unsure of what to order? Try the beef empanadas, flaky pastry dough filled with seasoned ground beef and served with a tasty pimento aioli. If you like seafood, opt for their pulpo, which is grilled octopus served over potato puree and a garlic-white wine reduction and paired with sweet peppers, grilled asparagus, and cherry tomatoes. As for the drink menu, Gustazo is the place to try rum. Their Hotel National is a signature drink at Havana's Hotel National de Cuba and is made with aged rum, pineapple, apricot, and lime.

20. DUMPLING CRAWL THROUGH CHINATOWN

Boston's Chinatown is a vital dining destination for anyone who considers themselves a true "foodie." Whether you are a local or just visiting, Chinatown is arguably one of the best food neighborhoods in the city. And if you're craving dumplings, Chinatown is where you need to be. One of Chinatown's staples is **Taiwan Café**. Here they serve an extensive selection of Taiwan and Sichuan dishes, but they are best known for their Taiwan-style pan-fried dumplings that are bursting with flavor. **Dumpling Café** is also a popular spot in Chinatown. Order their mini juicy buns (which are anything but mini) filled with flavorful broth, pork, and crab meat. I promise you won't be disappointed.

Eat Like a Local

21. EXPLORE EASTIE'S COLOMBIAN DINING SCENE

East Boston (or Eastie, as the local's call it), has a vibrant Colombian food scene. Head to this neighborhood for some of the best Colombian food in the city. **Melodias Restaurant** offers incredible seafood including their camarones al ajillo which are shrimp sautéed in a garlicky sauce. **La Casa Del Pandebono** not only sells delicious Colombian cheese bread, but features classic food items from Colombia as well as Mexico, Venezuela, and El Salvador. The bonito is a must-try item which comes with Colombian cheese bread, fried dough, an egg and chorizo scramble, cheese, and avocado. Finally, **La Abundancia Bakery & Restaurant** makes an incredible huevos revueltos (scrambled eggs) served with homemade arepas and queso.

22. SIP GREEK WINE

Named after the Greek word for wine, **Krasi** is a sophisticated Greek restaurant located in the heart of Back Bay. Their bar features an exclusively Greek wine list. Join their Wednesday night Wine Symposium and sample four carefully selected Greek wines. As with most wine, Greek grapes are meant for sipping alongside food. Krasi offers a variety of flavorful meze plates, charcuterie platters, and dips. The staff at Krasi have extensive knowledge of Mediterranean wine. They will happily make suggestions that will perfectly compliment your meal. Some of my favorite dishes include the tiropita rolls (fluffy rolls stuffed with halloumi and paired with honey butter), the aginara (a pan-fried artichoke surrounded by fried mint leaves, crispy garlic, and yogurt sauce), and the giouvetsi (a flavorful lamb osso buco paired with ripe tomatoes and orzo). Feeling extra hungry? Order the Feast of the Gods, which is one of every meze on the menu.

23. GET COTTON CANDY AT THE MEXICAN MAINSTAY

One of the city's most popular Mexican restaurants is **Lolita,** located in the Seaport. The best way to describe the décor at Lolita is "gothic chic." The restaurant is dimly lit with exposed brick walls, ornate red chandeliers, and giant stain-glass windows above the main bar. Oh, and skulls. There are skulls everywhere. The menu features a variety of Mexican classics, including a selection of tacos, quesadillas, nachos, and three kinds of guacamole. The tocino guacamole is a popular pick and includes chunks of smokey applewood bacon. Their cocktail menu offers a substantial tequila selection. Try a pitcher of margaritas or "frolitas" (frozen margaritas). Don't forget to order the churros for dessert. They are Nutella-glazed with caramelized banana ice cream and shaved Mexican chocolate. On a warm day, grab a seat outside along the Fort Point Channel for dinner with a view. Ready for a fun surprise? Your check will come with a giant cloud of cotton candy and pop rocks.

24. SPLURGE ON SUSHI

If you're feeling fancy and are willing to indulge on some of the best sushi in the city, consider making a reservation at **Uni**, located in The Eliot Hotel in Back Bay. Uni's menu offers an incredible roster of sushi rolls, sashimi, nigiri, and izakaya-inspired small plates courtesy of world-renowned chef Ken Oringer. Dive into a bowl of spicy wagyu beef dumplings or their west coast Uni spoon topped with caviar and quail egg. Every item on the menu is bursting with flavor and presented exquisitely. The restaurant also offers a private omakase experience for those showing up with a hearty appetite. Wash it all down with one of their creative cocktails. I highly suggest the Tipsy Dipsy, which consists of arette blanco, lime, wasabi, sugar snap pea, pineapple, and loomi.

25. SAMPLE SPANISH SMALL PLATES

One of Boston's most admired restaurants, **Toro**, is located in the South End and serves modern and traditional Spanish-style tapas. Start with one of their most popular dishes, grilled corn slathered in aioli, cheese, pepper, and lime, but don't be afraid to branch out and try their smoked duck drumettes or roasted bone marrow. The menu is almost entirely small dishes, except for a few paella options (which you should definitely order). Don't skimp out on dessert, either. Their scrumptious churros are paired with a rich chocolate sauce for dipping. Finally, their bar program is robust with fun cocktails, a fruity sangria, and some of the best local beers. Toro is a great spot to go with a group of friends. They have ample seating inside but, on warm nights, have a large outdoor patio space complete with string lights and fire pits.

26. TUNES AND TAPAS

Tres Gatos in Jamacia Plain is a unique piece of real estate because it's not only a restaurant, but a bookstore and record store combined into one. Tres Gatos is an eccentric and fun dining experience, located on the first floor of an old Victorian house. The bar is built into what was once someone's living room, high-top tables are situated in the old bedroom, and the book and record shop are in the back of the building. The menu at Tres Gatos changes seasonally and is inspired by Barcelona. Snack on albondigas (Mexican meatballs), patatas bravas, or their roasted bone marrow (which is to die for). The cocktail menu is equally unique. Sip on a Kitty's Got Claws, a mezcal-based drink made with house-infused pepper syrup, apricot, ginger, lemon, and peach juices.

27. TRY VIETNAMESE IN DORCHESTER

If you're looking for Vietnamese food, look no further than **Banh Mi Ba Le** in Dorchester. Banh Mi Ba Le is both a Vietnamese market and takeout restaurant that serves some of the best Vietnamese food in the city. It's most popular dish, the grilled beef banh mi, is marinated in lemongrass and is the perfect combination of salty and sweet. Their bread is baked in-house and is both crispy on the outside and pillowy-soft on the inside. But banh mi is not the only thing they are good at making. Banh Mi Ba Le offers a wide variety of traditional Vietnamese dishes ranging from soups to salad to rice bowls to fresh Vietnamese pastries. Wash everything down with passion fruit juice, a lychee smoothie, or their delicious Vietnamese coffee.

28. CRAFT COCKTAILS MEET CHINESE FOOD

Award-winning bartender, Ran Duan, owns **Blossom Bar**, a trendy tiki bar in Brookline that offers exotic drinks alongside traditional Sichuan fare. While the menu boasts rich, bold flavors (mainly due to the liberal use of garlic and chili peppers), it's the cocktail artistry worth experiencing. Many of the libations feature Asian-inspired ingredients such as lychee, yuzu, and chili oil, which complement the food menu. Sip on a Broken Spanish, a fantastic concoction of tequila, coconut, avocado, Thai basil, and a chapulines tajin rim, or a Tito Puente, a combination of rye, toasted coconut, East India sherry, and mezcal. If you're feeling adventurous, this is the perfect place to experiment with creative cocktails.

29. RAMEN IN BROOKLINE

Situated inside the Coolidge Corner Arcade in Brookline is **Ganko Ittetsu Ramen,** arguably one of the best ramen spots in the city. This small establishment should not be overlooked as it brings Sapporo-style ramen to Boston. This process requires caramelizing the sauce in a wok with vegetables before adding it to the broth. This gives the ramen a rich flavor that's worth every mouthful. The menu is small but specialized. Ganko Ittetsu offers six different styles of ramen in addition to a handful of appetizer specials. Their minimalist selection reflects the restaurant's dedication to perfecting the ramen they serve. Their noodles are custom-made in Japan, and their soy sauce and miso are produced by a Japanese microbrewery. For lighter ramen, try their Shio. If you're craving something spicier, try the Gankara Miso.

30. MORE IN COOLIDGE CORNER

Coolidge Corner in Brookline is a foodie's dream. From shawarma to deli sandwiches to artisan pizza to sushi, Coolidge Corner has something for everyone. Indulge in Japanese BBQ at **Gyu-Kaku** or order from an extensive sushi menu at **Genki Ya**. **Michael's Deli** has delicious matzah ball soup and authentic Jewish deli sandwiches. Looking for a chic cocktail bar? **Barcelona Wine Bar** is the place to be. Grab a beer on tap at **Hops N Scotch** if you'd prefer something more casual. The options are endless.

31. SEE AND BE SEEN

It's all about glitz and glam at **Yvonne's,** located in Downtown Crossing. This elegant restaurant and bar is known for its sharable plates and inventive shareable cocktails (such as an oversized Moscow Mule made to serve four). Yvonne's is an ideal venue for any occasion, whether it's a romantic dinner for two or a group outing, and it serves an exquisite seasonal menu. Consider ordering their chicken and quinoa meatballs or lazy lobster dumplings, which are unique and full of flavor. Their Supper Club dining space is adorned with antique crystal chandeliers, overstuffed tufted sofas, and ornate wallpaper. For a more exclusive and intimate dining experience, you can try to reserve a spot in The Gallery, which can only be accessed behind a secret bookshelf at the back of the lounge.

32. DINE LIKE A PARISIAN

If the name doesn't convince you, the menu certainly will. Located in Boston's South End is the most adorable Parisian-inspired bistro and wine bar, **Frenchie**. Come for brunch and order crepes or a croque madame. In the evening, consider a creamy onion soup or the steak frites. While the dining room is lined with beautiful floral wallpaper, the real treat is snagging a seat in their glass-enclosed conservatory lit by twinkling bistro lights. The restaurant's dreamy setting pairs perfectly with their delicious food menu.

33. ANOTHER SOUTH END FAVORITE

Nestled under a charming brownstone on Tremont Street in the South End is **MIDA**, a quaint, contemporary Italian eatery worth visiting if you're craving carbs. The space is warm and inviting and has incredible traditional Italian staples. Start your meal with their mouthwatering arancini balls filled with rice, San Marzano tomatoes, and fontina cheese. For an entree, you can't go wrong with their classic carbonara or short rib lasagna. Chef Douglass Williams has mastered the art of pasta making. He prides himself on using locally sourced ingredients as well as seasonal ingredients. End your evening with a slice of their tiramisu crafted to perfection. For those with a gluten allergy, gluten-free pasta is available upon request.

34. FARM-TO-TABLE AT ITS FINEST

Chef Charlie Foster and owner Kristin Canty are the dynamic duo behind **Woods Hill Pier 4**, a restaurant dedicated to farm-to-table dining and sustainable sourcing. Tucked away near the harbor in the Seaport, Woods Hill offers delicious, seasonal dishes using organic, non-GMO ingredients from local purveyors. Try the grilled Woods Hill Farm pork shoulder or the creste di gallo. The menu also has several items that can be gluten-free and dairy free. The bar menu also takes advantage of naturally sourced ingredients. For example, the Lavender Bee's Knees uses honey and lavender grown by Canty herself. Their rotating cocktail, Farmer's Whim, features fresh, seasonal produce from local farms. Their finely selected wine list emphasizes wines that are organic too.

35. SEASONAL FAVORITES IN SOMERVILLE

At the back of a hidden parking lot in Union Square in Somerville is an intimate restaurant called **Field & Vine**. The restaurant itself looks like a garden oasis with potted plants lining the windowsills and tree branches and vines hanging above the chef's counter. Field & Vine prides itself on a frequently rotating menu of seasonal and local fare. While this restaurant is not strictly vegetarian, vegetables do take center stage on their menu. Their roasted beets and blistered shishitos are decorated in a rich mixture of spices and citrusy juices. Pescatarians can enjoy exquisitely fresh raw seafood options such as crudo or ceviche. Just make sure to order their cheddar cornbread as an appetizer. It is the perfect combination of sweet and savory and comes with a side of miso butter.

36. EAT PASTA IN BOSTON'S LITTLE ITALY

Italian food reigns supreme in the North End. This is Boston's version of Little Italy and the place to be if you're looking for the perfect pasta dish. Take a stroll along Hanover Street, and you will be graced with many great options. **Carmelina's** serves traditional Sicilian comfort food with a Mediterranean twist. Order their Sunday Macaroni which includes meatballs, beef rib, and Sulmona sausage in a savory tomato sauce, a dollop of whipped ricotta, and served over homemade rigatoni. Their wine menu also tells you what food pairs best with each glass. **Trattoria il Panino** is another excellent option offering innovative Neapolitan dishes. Start with their fried zucchini flowers and then indulge in a bowl of the paccheri al ragu rigatoni covered in a slow-cooked lamb, beef, veal, and pork ragu. Finally, **Mamma Maria** offers old-school Italian dishes in a romantic townhouse with a white-tablecloth ambiance. Order their Lobster Pasta which combines juicy Maine lobster and Venetian-style agnolotti pasta.

37. SIP ON AN ESPRESSO MARTINI

Nothing is better than a post-dinner espresso martini after a carb-filled pasta feast. While **Bricco** in the North End has incredible Italian food, it also makes the most famous espresso martini in the city. This critically acclaimed cocktail is made with Absolut vanilla vodka, Kahlúa, Disaronno, Baileys, Frangelico, and fresh espresso. Each martini arrives with a raw sugar and cocoa covered rim and three espresso beans inside. All the flavors complement each other, so you aren't left with an overpowering taste of vodka or espresso. It is rich, smooth, and utterly delightful. Why stop at just one?

38. CANNOLI CRAWL THROUGH THE NORTH END

If you are craving an after-dinner treat, consider visiting one of the North End's bakeries to snag a cannoli. **Modern Pastry** and **Mike's Pastry** are local favorites for these cream-filled pastries, which is evident from their competing long lines. However, tucked away one block behind Hanover Street is another hidden gem, **Bova's Bakery**. This shop is rarely crowded and stays open later than the other bakeries in the neighborhood. Regardless of which bakery you choose, you won't be disappointed. All three locations offer an array of Italian cookies and pastries, and Mike's offers gelato, making it a one-stop shop for family desserts.

39. GRAB A PINT

Located in Boston's Seaport is **Harpoon Brewery**, which has been a neighborhood staple for more than 30 years. Come here to enjoy IPAs, stouts, and more. Some of their most popular flavors include the standard Harpoon IPA (an Indian Pale Ale), Harpoon Camp Wannamango (a sweet mango flavored pale ale), and Harpoon Flannel Fridays (a hoppy amber ale with notes of citrus and caramel). Grab a seat at a table in their beer hall and enjoy a brew and a giant pretzel. If you're visiting on the weekend, pay $10 for a 50-minute brewery tour for a walk through the brewery. Harpoon hosts various fun-filled events throughout the year, so keep an eye on their website for more information.

40. CHEERS TO MORE BEER!

Harpoon is not the only beer hall in the city. In fact, Boston has a thriving beer culture. Whether you enjoy IPAs, lagers, stouts, or sours, there is an option for everyone. **Trillium** brewery has a multi-level pub in Fort Point and a seasonal beer garden on the Greenway downtown. Their flagship beer, the Congress Street IPA, is an American IPA that features notes of pine, citrus, pineapple, and melon. They also have a rotating selection of rich dessert stouts infused with coffee, vanilla, and even cocoa. Another popular brewery is **Night Shift Brewing**, located in Everett. More recently, they opened a taproom downtown near the TD Garden. Seasonally, they have a pop-up beer garden called Owl's Nest near the Esplanade. One of their more popular beers is the Whirlpool, a dry-hopped New England-style pale with a nose of peach and citrus. Finally, **Lamplighter's** taproom can be found in Cambridge, offering a selection of barrel-aged sours and other experimental brews. Come here and try Rabbit Rabbit, a double dry-hopped Double IPA bursting with bold flavor.

41. EXPERIENCE COCKTAIL ARTISTRY

If beer isn't your thing, there are plenty of terrific cocktail bars scattered through the city. Barbara Lynch's craft cocktail bar called **Drink** in South Boston's Fort Point neighborhood is one you should not miss. For years, the establishment had no menu. Instead, its mixologists relied on their patrons to tell them what spirit they liked and what flavors they were craving. Within a few years, Drink became not only one of the most well-respected bars in the city but in 2013, was named the "World's Best Cocktail Bar." While the restaurant recently implemented a small drink menu, guests can still use the "tell me what you want" approach and order a customized libation from the bar. The space is small yet inviting. Its décor is industrial chic with exposed brick walls and warehouse light fixtures, creating a modern yet cozy atmosphere to enjoy a delicious hand-crafted cocktail.

42. VISIT A SPEAKEASY

Hidden behind an unmarked door down an alley in Boston's Leather District is **Offsuit**. This swanky speakeasy offers an intimate experience, where burgundy-colored walls, plush leather loveseats, and dimly lit chandeliers impart a mysterious vibe you'd expect from a Prohibition-era speakeasy. The cocktail list is "no-frills – no fuss" and offers classics, including an espresso martini, dirty martini, and gimlet, as well as more creative libations such as an Isolated Incident (tequila, pineapple, lemon, Santa Teresa 1796, ancho reyes and coffee bitters). The space is small and can only seat 20 guests, so reservations are required and limited to 90 minutes. Between the unbelievable drink menu and unforgettable ambiance, Offsuit is worth a visit.

43. STOP AT FENWAY FOR A FRANK

I think it goes without saying that hot dogs are the perfect baseball snack. They go hand in hand, like peanut butter and jelly or cookies and milk. They are tasty and filling and can be decorated with an assortment of toppings, from chili and cheese, sauerkraut or ketchup and mustard. But the Fenway Frank is unlike other ballpark hot dogs. While competitors are steamed or grilled, Fenway boils *and* grills their franks, helping them retain their juiciness. They are also made of a concoction of spices and meats to give them a bolder flavor. Needless to say, Fenway Franks are a Boston staple, and if you find yourself at a Red Sox game, you should definitely purchase this fan favorite.

44. TASTE TEST AT A FOOD MARKET

Time Out Market brings the best of the city's cuisines and cocktails to one location. Time Out Market has everything from pizza to tacos to donuts to dumplings. You can choose from 15 different dining options under one roof. Craving something savory? Grab the birria tacos from **Taqueria el Barrio** or the karaage chicken and waffle fries from **Ms. Clucks Deluxe Chicken & Dumplings**. If you're looking for something sweet, try the Nutella La Land crepe from Say Coffee Co. or an artisanal Italian gelato from **Gelato & Chill**. Wash things down at the Time Out Market Bar, which offers a carefully curated selection of international wines, fine beers, and cocktails. Time Out Market is located in Fenway and offers first-come, first-serve seating.

45. MORE MARKET MUNCHIES

Bow Market in Somerville is a one-stop shop for a plethora of drinking and dining destinations for every kind of palette. Pay a visit to **Tanám**, which offers Filipino-American cuisine. Order their double-fried chicken wings or a pork spring roll. If you prefer plant-based food, try **Saus**, which excels in the art of vegetarian comfort food. Their award-winning poutine is excellent. For dessert, pop over to **Maca** which makes colorful and scrumptious macarons. Wash it all down with a cold beer from **Remnant Brewing** or a glass of wine from **Rebel Rebel**. Bow Market is also home to a variety of retail shops so you can tackle some shopping after you eat.

46. DON'T FORGET FOOD TRUCKS

Sometimes you don't have time for a full sit-down meal. And that's okay. That's why food trucks are an excellent grab-and-go option. The Greenway in Downtown Boston has a surplus of fantastic food trucks that cater to a range of appetites. Many other trucks can be found in Allston, Cambridge, and Brookline too. For comfort food, consider **Roxy's Grilled Cheese and Burgers**. Grab an ooey-gooey grilled cheese sandwich with a side of hearty tomato soup. Roxy's food truck can be found in Allston. **Bon Me** is a fantastic option for Vietnamese sandwiches and scallion pancakes. **Chicken and Rice Guys** is excellent for a lamb gyro or halal chicken with a side of rice. And don't forget about dessert! **The Cookie Monstah** food truck offers cookies, cakes, and ice cream sandwiches. Their newest menu option, the Cookie Quake, is a combo of cookies and ice cream blended into milkshake perfection. Bon Me, Chicken and Rice Guys and The Cookie Monstah can all be found in the Greenway.

47. GO TO THE PLACE WHERE "EVERYBODY KNOWS YOUR NAME"

Experience the bar that inspired one of the most beloved American sitcoms of all time, *Cheers*. Previously known as the Bull & Finch Pub, **Cheers on Beacon Hill** became the original inspiration for the setting of *Cheers*. The menu features traditional pub fare items named after the show's main characters. Patrons with a large appetite can take on the "Norm Burger Challenge" and attempt to finish a double-decker burger to earn a spot on their wall of fame. Feeling nostalgic? Head upstairs to see a replica of the original TV set or the gift shop for memorabilia. Cheers is located on Beacon Street across from the Boston Common in Boston's beautiful Beacon Hill neighborhood.

48. TAKE A COOKING CLASS

Eataly in Back Bay is your one-stop shop for anything Italian. This 45,000-square-foot food emporium houses three restaurants, five bars, takeaway counters, a huge market, and a separate space for cooking classes. Their marketplace offers an assortment of fresh loaves of bread, different kinds of pasta, cheese, wines, and more. Head to La Pizza & La Pasta for authentic Neapolitan pizza and perfectly cooked pasta. The tagliatelle pasta with beef brisket ragu is to die for. If you prefer seasonal fare, head upstairs to their rooftop restaurant, Terra. This restaurant features a variety of grill-based food items that are locally sourced. Finally, if you're more hands-on culinary experience, take a cooking class at **La Scuola di Eataly**, where you'll get the chance to make your own pasta!

49. VISIT THE OLDEST RESTAURANT IN THE CITY

From the Boston Tea Party to Paul Revere's midnight ride, the city of Boston is full of history. But what some people don't know is that Boston is also home to one of the oldest operating restaurants in America: **Union Oyster House**. While many great restaurants serve seafood, this one doubles as a National Historic Landmark. In 1826, the restaurant opened its doors to diners and continues to draw a considerable crowd for its clam chowder, crispy calamari, and, of course, freshly shucked oysters. While you enjoy your meal, you'll be in view of John F. Kennedy's favorite booth and the oyster bar where Daniel Webster drank his daily tumbler of brandy and water. Union Oyster House is located between Faneuil Hall and the North End along the Freedom Trail, making it an easy stop for tourists.

50. END WITH SOME HISTORY

Located in downtown Boston, **Quincy Market** was built in the early 1800s to accommodate an influx of vendors to Faneuil Hall. In fact, it was Boston's first major construction project after officially becoming a city in 1822. Today, locals consider it to be a quintessential tourist trap, but there are some decent food options inside. After window shopping in Faneuil Hall, pop into Quincy Market's food hall to restore your energy. Here you can find New England favorites like fried seafood and fries at the **Fisherman's Net** or a warm bowl of clam chowder at Boston **Chowda Co**. If you're craving meat, order an Italian sausage or Portuguese kielbasa at the Dog House. For something sweet, snag an M&M cookie at **Carol Ann Bake Shop**. If anything, Quincy Market is dripping in history, so it's worth checking off your to-do list.

Eat Like a Local

WHY YOU SHOULD B OOK THIS TRIP

BOSTON IS RICH IN HISTORY

Whether you're a US history buff or not, Boston is filled with American historical sites to see. You can follow the Freedom Trail (marked by red brick markers throughout the city) and visit the site of the Boston Massacre, the USS Constitution, the Paul Revere House, and more. There are 16 landmarks in total, and the self-guided walking tour only takes a few hours. Boston is also home to the Bunker Hill Monument and the Old State House, the oldest surviving public building in the city. It is also where the Declaration of Independence was read in 1776.

Boston is also home to Harvard University, the United States' oldest higher education institution. Visitors can stroll through the campus established in 1636 free of charge. On the University's main campus, located on Harvard Yard in Cambridge, you can find Massachusetts Hall, where several of the founding fathers (Samuel Adams, John Hancock, Elbridge Gerry, and James Otis) slept while attending classes at the university.

While the city continues to evolve, Boston will always embrace its historic past.

BOSTON HAS SO MUCH CHARM

Everywhere you look, beautiful historic architecture coexists with 21st-century design. You can walk down charming cobblestone streets and tree-lined avenues on the same day as exploring the modern and thriving seaport harbor. Neighborhoods like Beacon Hill, Back Bay, and the South End are adorned with adorable brownstone buildings that give the city its quintessential New England charm. In fact, Acorn Street in Beacon Hill is one of the most photographed streets in the country.

The Charles River runs gallantly through the city, separating Boston from Cambridge. On any given day, you can see people walking, biking, or rollerblading along the water. Some people even set up their own hammocks by the river so they can enjoy a good book with a view. There are options to rent kayaks, sailboats, and paddleboards so you can enjoy breathtaking views of the city from the riverbanks.

Finally, Boston also has a lot of vegetation for a metropolitan city. From the Boston Public Garden to the Charles River Esplanade to the Greenway, there is no shortage of greenery. Visit during the Fall, and you can see Boston's Autumn foliage illuminate the city.

BOSTON LOVES ITS SPORTS TEAMS

Did you know that Fenway Park is the oldest ballpark in America? It has been home to the Boston Red Sox since 1912. Whether or not you're a sports fanatic, Boston's sports scene is definitely one to experience. Stop by a baseball game at Fenway Park and sing along to Neil Diamond's famous song "Sweet Caroline" during the eight inning, or buy tickets to a basketball game at TD Garden and watch the Celtics play. If there are no games during your visit, Fenway also offers scheduled park tours.

Another sports-related site worth seeing is the Boston Marathon Finish Line on Boylston Street, which can be seen year-round. Every year in April, tens of thousands of runners finish the Boston Marathon, the world's oldest marathon dating back to 1897. Hundreds of thousands of spectators gather around the sidelines each year to cheer on the runners. Every year the marathon brings the city together with pride, especially since the attack in 2013 that created the unity phrase, "Boston Strong."

BONUS: BOSTON SLANG WORDS YOU SHOULD KNOW

Chowda

Short for Clam Chowder, which you most certainly should order if you're visiting Boston.

How to use it in a sentence: "I'd like a lobster roll and a side of clam chowda."

Dunks

They say that America runs on Dunkin', but Boston *really* runs on Dunkin'. Dunks is a nickname for Dunkin' Donuts.

How to use it in a sentence: "I'm running to Dunks, what do you want to drink?"

Frappe

Pronounced as "frap" and not "frap-ay," this refers to a milkshake made with milk, syrup, *and* ice cream. This is not to be confused with a milkshake, which is just syrup and milk.

How to use it in a sentence: "He made the best vanilla frappe."

The Garden

Short for TD Garden, the large arena where the Bruins and Celtics play.

How to use it in a sentence: "I'm headed to the Garden tonight to watch the Celtics play."

Eat Like a Local

Green Monstah

Aka the Green Monster, which refers to the left field wall in Fenway Park.

How to use it in a sentence: "Did you see him hit that ball over the Green Monstah?"

Grinder

Pronounced as "grinah" and not grinder, this refers to a sandwich or a hoagie.

How to use it in a sentence: "I'm gonna pick up a couple of grinders for lunch."

Packie

A liquor store. Massachusetts law requires alcohol to be sold in sealed packages outside of the bottle, which is how this term came about. Packie is short for "package store."

How to use it in a sentence: "What do you want to drink? I'm stopping at the packie."

Supper

Most people call this dinner, but Supper refers to the third meal of the day.

How to use it in a sentence: "What are we having for supper tonight?"

Townie

A name for someone who grew up and still lives in a certain neighborhood of Boston.

How to use it in a sentence: "The bar was packed with townies."

Wicked Pissah

While this may sound like an insult, it is quite the opposite. "Wicked pissah" refers to something that is very cool.

How to use it in a sentence: "Your new car is a wicked pissah!"

READ OTHER BOOKS BY CZYK PUBLISHING

Eat Like a Local United States Cities & Towns

Eat Like a Local United States

Eat Like a Local- Oklahoma: Oklahoma Food Guide

Eat Like a Local- North Carolina: North Carolina Food Guide

Eat Like a Local- New York City: New York City Food Guide

Children's Book: Charlie the Cavalier Travels the World by Lisa Rusczyk

Eat Like a Local

Follow *Eat Like a Local* on Amazon.
Join our mailing list for new books

http://bit.ly/EatLikeaLocalbooks

CZYKPublishing.com

Printed in Great Britain
by Amazon